THE MORNING WATCH

THE MORNING WATCH

Andrew Murray

Compiled & Editted By
Cyril Opoku

Copyright © 2014. All Rights Reserved.

Quest Publications

A PRODUCTION OF

Quest Publications
http://questpub.questforgod.org

This book is available for download on Quest Publications' website and through many booksellers. Copying and distribution is prohibited without prior permission from the Author.

Print copies can be ordered through Quest Publications and many other online book retailers. To order in bulk, send an email to Quest Publications for a special discounted price.

Email to: info@questforgod.org.

Because of the dynamic nature of the Internet, any web addresses or links contained in this book may have changed since publication and may no longer be valid.

Rev. Date: 14-Dec-14

ISBN-13: 978-1505544466
ISBN-10: 1505544467

This book may not be copied or reprinted for commercial gain or profit. The use of short quotations or occasional page copying for personal or group study is permitted and encouraged. Permission will be granted upon request.

Unless otherwise stated, all scripture quotations are taken from the King James Version. Public Domain.

CONTENTS

Begin the Day with Prayer—viii

Abraham And The Morning Watch—1

Jacob And The Morning Watch—4

Victory In The Morning Watch—7

The Law Of The Manna —10

The Morning Watch And The Law Of God—13

The Morning Burnt Offering —16

The Incense Of Sweet Spices—19

The Morning Watch And Sin Confession—22

Fire Upon The Altar—25

The Morning Watch And Consecration—28

Joshua And The Morning Watch—31

The Light Of The Morning—34

Job And The Morning Watch—37

A Visit From God Every Morning—40

Surely Now He Will Awake For Thee—43

Thou Shalt Be As The Morning—46

My Voice Shalt Thou Hear In The Morning—49

Joyful Morning Prayer—52

Early Will I Seek Thee—55

In The Morning Shall My Prayer Prevent Thee—58

Thy Lovingkindness Is Better Than Life—61

Satisfy Us Early With Thy Mercy—64

Showing Forth His Lovingkindness In The Morning—67

Seeking God Early—70

Be Thou My Arm Every Morning—73

Awaken Mine Ear Every Morning—76

New Mercies Every Morning—79

The Just Lord and His Judgments Every Morning—82

Secret Communion With God—85

Great Lessons Spring From The Morning Watch—88

The Secret Of Early Rising—91

The Morning Watch in the Life of Obedience.—94

NOTES ON THE MORNING WATCH.—108

Biography of Andrew Murray—115

FOREWORD

Begin the Day with Prayer

I ought to pray before seeing any one. Often when I sleep long, or meet with others early, it is eleven or twelve o'clock before I begin secret prayer. This is a wretched system. It is unscriptural. Christ arose before day and went into a solitary place. David says: "Early will I seek thee"; "Thou shalt early hear my voice." Family prayer loses much of its power and sweetness, and I can do no good to those who come to seek from me. The conscience feels guilty, the soul unfed, the lamp not trimmed. Then when in secret prayer the soul is often out of tune, I feel it is far better to begin with God -- to see his face first, to get my soul near him before it is near another.
—Robert Murray McCheyne

FOREWORD—*Begin The Day With Prayer*

THE men who have done the most for God in this world have been early on their knees. He who fritters away the early morning, its opportunity and freshness, in other pursuits than seeking God will make poor headway seeking him the rest of the day. If God is not first in our thoughts and efforts in the morning, he will be in the last place the remainder of the day.

Behind this early rising and early praying is the ardent desire which presses us into this pursuit after God. Morning listlessness is the index to a listless heart. The heart which is behindhand in seeking God in the morning has lost its relish for God. David's heart was ardent after God. He hungered and thirsted after God, and so he sought God early, before daylight. The bed and sleep could not chain his soul in its eagerness after God. Christ longed for communion with God; and so, rising a great while before day, he would go out into the mountain to pray. The disciples, when fully awake and ashamed of their indulgence, would know where to find him. We might go through the list of men who have mightily impressed the world for God, and we would find them early after God.

A desire for God which cannot break the chains of

sleep is a weak thing and will do but little good for God after it has indulged itself fully. The desire for God that keeps so far behind the devil and the world at the beginning of the day will never catch up.

It is not simply the getting up that puts men to the front and makes them captain generals in God's hosts, but it is the ardent desire which stirs and breaks all self-indulgent chains. But the getting up gives vent, increase, and strength to the desire. If they had lain in bed and indulged themselves, the desire would have been quenched. The desire aroused them and put them on the stretch for God, and this heeding and acting on the call gave their faith its grasp on God and gave to their hearts the sweetest and fullest revelation of God, and this strength of faith and fullness of revelation made them saints by eminence, and the halo of their sainthood has come down to us, and we have entered on the enjoyment of their conquests. But we take our fill in enjoyment, and not in productions. We build their tombs and write their epitaphs, but are careful not to follow their examples.

We need a generation of preachers who seek God and seek him early, who give the freshness and dew of effort to God, and secure in return the freshness

FOREWORD—*Begin The Day With Prayer*

and fullness of his power that he may be as the dew to them, full of gladness and strength, through all the heat and labor of the day. Our laziness after God is our crying sin. The children of this world are far wiser than we. They are at it early and late. We do not seek God with ardor and diligence. <u>No man gets God who does not follow hard after him, and no soul follows hard after God who is not after him in early morn.</u>

Edward McKendree Bounds (1835-1913)
Taken from the Classic, Power Through Prayer

1

Abraham And The Morning Watch

"And Abraham rose up early in the morning."

(Gen. 21:14 and Gen. 22:3.)

Twice we find this said of Abraham, both times in reference to what was painful to him. The first time it was to send away his son Ishmael from his home (21:14), and the second time to face the still harder task of offering up Isaac. His early rising was the token of his whole-hearted willingness to do the will of God.

How glorious was the reward of his early rising which Abraham received. It brought him on the third day to the mountains where the Lord appeared unto him—and favour followed upon his obedience. He gave him back his son as from the dead. He confirmed to him the promise of blessing: "In blessing I will bless thee, and in multiplying I will multiply thy seed". Abraham learns to know his God as the worker of wonders of whom he could say, "The Lord will provide."

My brother! If ever a day comes when you are called upon to do what seems to you hard and difficult, do as Abraham did. <u>Arise in the morning hour to meet your God in a spirit of willingness to accomplish only His will.</u> If you desire to walk in Abraham's footsteps, and to sacrifice all to God, yea, even what is dearest, then go to meet God in the early morning hour. To you, too, on rising early, He will reveal Himself as the Lord and will provide. To you, too, will He confirm it by an oath, saying, "In blessing I will bless thee, and in multiplying I will multiply thy seed." Thus was Abraham rewarded for that early rising.

1—Abraham And The Morning Watch

If ever a day comes when you are called upon to do what seems to you hard and difficult, do as Abraham did. Arise in the morning hour to meet your God…

2

Jacob And The Morning Watch

"And Jacob rose up early in the morning,"

(Gen. 28:19.)

The Lord had appeared to Jacob at Bethel in the night. He had seen the glorious heavenly ladder with God the Lord standing above it. He had received from God the promise that He would be with him and would never leave him until He had accomplished all that He had promised. Then Jacob rose up early in the morning and vowed a vow of which the gist was, 'The Lord shall be my God' (Gen. 28:21).

Child of God! Christ is the true heavenly ladder; from above it God speaks to thee in the darkest night, I will be with thee and will not leave thee. Dost thou not think that every morning summons thee to say with Jacob: "The Lord shall be my God"?

2—Jacob And The Morning Watch

Can you imagine a more glorious beginning of the day? You pass every night under the protection of Jacob's God, is it not right that you should begin each morning with Jacob's vow?

Make a habit of being alone with God the first hour of the morning. Consider what He is to you through Christ. Meditate on the wonderful promise He has given you of His continual presence and His unchangeable faithfulness. Listen while He says to you: "I am with thee and will not leave thee." Take time so by faith to appropriate this promise that your whole soul knows that God Himself has spoken these words to you. Say then, "The Lord shall be my God." Jacob rose up early in the morning to utter that vow; do thou likewise.

MAKE A HABIT OF BEING ALONE WITH GOD THE FIRST HOUR OF THE MORNING..SAY THEN, "THE LORD SHALL BE MY GOD." JACOB ROSE UP EARLY IN THE MORNING TO UTTER THAT VOW; DO THOU LIKEWISE.

3

Victory In The Morning Watch

"And it came to pass that in the morning watch the Lord looked unto the hosts of the Egyptians through the pillar of fire and of the cloud, and troubled the host of the Egyptians. And Moses stretched forth his hand over the sea and the sea returned to his strength when the morning appeared...and the Lord overthrew the Egyptians in the midst of the sea."

(Exod. 14:24, 27.)

It was in the early morning that the Lord gave unto Israel complete victory over their enemies in fulfilment of the promise made the previous day, "The Egyptians whom ye have seen today, ye shall see them again no more for ever" (v. 13). Then, too, my soul shall discover that the morning is still God's chosen time for giving His children the victory over their enemies. "This is the victory which overcometh the world, even our faith."

Looking up to God in the quiet of the morning, Faith can find time to lay strong hold upon Him, and meditating upon and appropriating His influence, find the firm ground upon which the fulfilment of every promise may be expected, through surrender to Christ in Whom the victory over the world and every foe has already been accomplished. Faith finds in Christ the strength for all the conflicts it must wage. "Fear ye not, stand still and see the salvation of the Lord" these words which heralded the deliverance of that morning teach us what should be our expectation and our frame of mind at the beginning of every morning. Yea, Lord, when I behold mine enemies this day I will not fear but" stand still and see the salvation of the Lord." Christian, be vigilant of the morning watch. "The Lord shall fight for you and ye shall hold your peace." Yea, Amen, my soul is continually quiet before God.

3—Victory In The Morning Watch

THE MORNING IS STILL GOD'S CHOSEN TIME FOR GIVING HIS CHILDREN THE VICTORY OVER THEIR ENEMIES.

4

The Law Of The Manna

"In the morning ye shall be filled with bread, and ye shall know that I am the Lord your God. And they gathered it every morning, and when the sun waxed hot it melted."

(Exod. 16:12, 21.)

In these verses we have the law of the manna. The Lord would send it in the morning: in the morning it was to be collected. He who neglected to gather his manna in the morning would have to go hungry the whole day long. All this is a foreshadowing of our blessed Saviour. He Himself is the bread from Heaven, the hidden manna. It is in the morning that the believer, even though he be one of the weakest, must draw nigh to God to receive his portion for the day. The reading of the Word is not all that he has to do, the Word is the vessel in which the bread of life is served; he must

4—The Law Of The Manna

not only read and meditate upon the Word; he must know and accept the living Christ as his bread of life. Jesus is the "hidden manna." Neither is it enough to pray; prayer is seeking after the manna; he must be sure actually to find the Bread of Life and carry it with him during the day as his food and source of strength.

This is accomplished by faith. Faith sees and finds and takes and eats. By faith I look up in the morning to Jesus as my life. By faith I surrender myself, in the full sense of His love to me, in that He will be my life throughout the day. I tarry until my soul has the full assurance of this. By faith I thank the Lord that I may possess Him for the whole day and I go out into the heat of the day in the rest and gladness of the assurance that Jesus is my Life for this day.

THE MANNA—THE LORD WOULD SEND IT IN THE MORNING: IN THE MORNING IT WAS TO BE COLLECTED. HE WHO NEGLECTED TO GATHER HIS MANNA IN THE MORNING WOULD HAVE TO GO HUNGRY THE WHOLE DAY LONG.

5

The Morning Watch And The Law Of God

"And it came to pass on the third day in the morning that there were thunders and lightnings...Moses brought forth the people out of the camp to meet with God...And when the voice of the trumpet sounded long and waxed louder and louder, Moses spake and God answered him by a voice."

(Exod. 19:16-19.)

What a memorable day for Moses and for Israel and for all mankind—the day on which the Law was promulgated! The day begins at the morning hour when Moses led out the people to meet with God, and spake with God, and God answered him.

The law of God must be renewed every day in our hearts. The inward law of the Spirit is a living law, and is every day renewed and kept in force from heaven. If I wish to have this experience during the day, I must begin this morning as Moses did go to meet with God, and speak with Him, and wait for His answer.

To meet with God! Prepare, my soul, to meet thy God. God had said to Moses, "Sanctify them against the morrow, for I will come unto thee." He who would meet with God must purify and sanctify himself, lay aside all that is sinful with a humble confession of guilt; offer thyself to God a holy sacrifice. Give thyself with fear and reverence into the hands of the great and holy God, that He may be Lord over you this day. Prepare to meet Him. Be content with nothing less. Take time, be still before Him, let faith await God. He will come unto thee. And when thou hast met with Him, speak unto Him and let Him answer thee. Let His Word be, through the Holy Spirit, His voice in thy soul. The morning whereon thou hast met with Him will be the beginning of a blessed day.

5—The Morning Watch And The Law Of God

When thou hast met with Him, speak unto Him and let Him answer thee. Let His Word be, through the Holy Spirit, His voice in thy soul.

6

The Morning Burnt Offering

"The one lamb thou shalt offer in the morning and the other lamb thou shalt offer at even... This shall be a continual burnt offering throughout your generations...before the Lord, where I will meet you to speak there unto thee."

(Exod. 29:39, 42.)

Beside the continual burnt offering in the morning which was for a "continual burnt offering" (Num. 28:10), the sin offering foreshadowed Christ alone; the thank offering has reference to us, and what we bring to God; the burnt offering to Christ and also to us. The distinguishing mark of the burnt offering was that it was placed whole upon the altar, so as to rise up wholly to God in the fire. Other offerings were brought from time to time.

6—The Morning Burnt Offering

The morning burnt offering had to be brought each day, it was the beginning of the service of God for that day, and the Christian, too, should bring his burnt offering every morning. What does this mean? Every morning he comes to God looking to the Lamb of God offered for his sin. He sees how Jesus gave Himself a whole burnt offering to God, and learns how he must do it, too; because he is one with Christ even in His death, because he must be a perfect copy of his Lord, because the same Spirit dwells in him, he lays himself upon the altar of Christ's merit as a living, holy sacrifice, well-pleasing unto God; he sacrifices himself entirely to God. Christian, it is a great thing to accomplish this sacrifice every morning, but it is a glorious thing, the secret of a blessed day.

The fire of the Spirit descends upon such a sacrifice. Take time in silence and solitude until you are assured, and can say, "My offering is upon the altar acceptable unto the Father, and the fire shall consume it."

THE MORNING BURNT OFFERING HAD TO BE BROUGHT EACH DAY, IT WAS THE BEGINNING OF THE SERVICE OF GOD FOR THAT DAY, AND THE CHRISTIAN, TOO, SHOULD BRING HIS BURNT OFFERING EVERY MORNING.

7

The Incense Of Sweet Spices

"And thou shalt overlay it (the altar) with pure gold...and Aaron shall burn thereon incense of sweet spices every morning; when he dresseth the lamps he shall burn it."

(Exod. 30:3, 7.)

The "incense of sweet spices" signifies prayer. "Let my prayer be set forth as incense before Thee." (Psa. 141:2.) "And there was given unto him (the angel) much incense that he should add it unto the prayers of all the saints upon the golden altar that was before the throne." (Rev. 3:1.)

The prayer that comes up to God through the great High Priest is to Him a sweet savour. Every morning that incense had to be burnt by the priests while the house of God was filled with the fragrance. This is what I, too, must do as a priest of God—I am the temple of God. The whole heart must be filled with the sweet savour of the prayer and thanksgiving which I offer up to God every morning. One thing, above all, is necessary to this end. I must know that my prayers are acceptable to the Father. The Holy Spirit will give me inward assurance of this. I must take time before my prayer, and during prayer, and after prayer, to realize, by faith, God's love and favour. I must, by faith, become conscious of my unity with Christ. I must surrender myself to the purpose of walking in that union. I must suffer the Holy Spirit to breathe into me the living assurance that my Father verily looks upon my prayer with pleasure.

This will fill me with the strength to burn my incense of sweet spices every morning, to send up prayers inspired by the Holy Spirit. Then I can go forth to walk as a priest before God the whole day.

7—The Incense Of Sweet Spices

"Fill me with the strength to burn my incense of sweet spices every morning, to send up prayers inspired by the Holy Spirit."

8

The Morning Watch And Sin Confession

"And Moses rose up early in the morning and went up unto Mount Sinai...And the Lord... stood with him there and proclaimed the name of the Lord...and Moses made haste and bowed his head toward the earth and worshipped."

(Exod. 34:4-5, 8.)

The previous occasion on which Moses went to meet the Lord in the morning was the time of the promulgation of the Law when God was to reveal Himself as the Holy One. The meeting with which we are now concerned was after the transgression of the Law when God was to reveal Himself as the Merciful One (see verses 6 and 7). These two elements should always be united in the morning worship of the Child of God. In our communion with God one morning may be more concerned with surrender in obedience to His will,

8—The Morning Watch And Sin Confession

but the background of all will be the Redeeming Grace which accepts us and makes us fit for His service. Another morning we may be more drawn to worship God as the Merciful and Gracious One, but behind this will be the knowledge of the condition that we are restored to His favour in order to do what is His good pleasure.

Christian, if thou wouldst serve God aright, learn to know Him aright. Arise out of the low lying plains of your own thoughts about Him. Climb the mountain where God will stand beside you and proclaim the Name of the Lord. Rise up early in the morning and come with your confession of laws transgressed, and bring the fleshy tables of your heart, and God will write thereon His Name and His Law, and when you bow your head and worship, as Moses did that early morning upon the mountain, you will receive, like him, power to plead as an intercessor for God's people and receive God's answer, "Behold, I make a covenant: before all thy people I will do marvels".

CHRISTIAN, IF THOU WOULDST SERVE GOD ARIGHT, LEARN TO KNOW HIM ARIGHT...RISE UP EARLY IN THE MORNING AND COME WITH YOUR CONFESSION OF LAWS TRANSGRESSED... '

9

Fire Upon The Altar

"And the fire upon the altar shall be kept burning thereon; it shall not go out; and the priest shall burn wood upon it every morning."

(Lev. 6:12.)

All acknowledge that the fire upon the altar is the type of the Holy Spirit. The sacrifice upon the altar of burnt offering, and the sweet-smelling spices upon the altar of incense, all were to be consumed by the fire and carried up to Heaven in smoke. So only may the sacrifice whereby I offer myself up to God every morning, and the incense of my prayers be well pleasing unto God, when they are borne by the Holy Spirit to Heaven. Then it is "an acceptable sacrifice", being sanctified by the Holy Spirit.

And therefore the fire upon the Altar must always be kept burning. And the appointed time is the morning; the priest shall burn wood upon it every morning. The Christian who neglects this duty in the morning will soon discover that he cannot find time for it in the course of the day. Let us learn to do this in the morning. The wood needful to keep the fire of the Spirit burning is God's Word. Let us see to it that these two things are done every morning: first, we must gather and pile the wood; secondly, we must wait for the fire of the Spirit to set it alight. Through faith and a truthful waiting upon God, we must have the inward assurance that the Holy Spirit, the fire of God, is burning within us. Then our sacrifice of ourselves and our prayers will be a sweet savour, acceptable to God in Christ.

9—Fire Upon The Altar

The sacrifice whereby I offer myself up to God every morning, and the incense of my prayers [may] be well pleasing unto God when they are borne by the Holy Spirit to Heaven.

10

The Morning Watch And Consecration

"In the morning the Lord will show who are His, and who is holy, and will cause him to come near unto Him, even him whom He shall choose will He cause to come near unto Him."

(Num. 16:5.)

The Lord had chosen Aaron and his sons to be His, and had consecrated them as priests" to come near unto Him." Korah and others complained of this, and said that this was self-exaltation; that on the contrary the whole nation was holy. Moses replied that God would decide. He would show early in the morning who were His.

Now every believer is a priest, chosen to come near unto God, but he cannot rightly grasp this or experience the power of it in his life unless the Lord make it known unto him. God is very willing to do

10—The Morning Watch And Consecration

this anew every morning in the quietness of the early morning. His will is to give you, through the Spirit, the heavenly assurance that you are His, His own possession, which He has chosen and separated to Himself. You are one holy in Christ, whom He will cause to come near unto Him, whom He will draw near unto Himself to commune with Him as an intercessor for the people. This God will show you through His holy Spirit.

Oh, Christian, build not, like Korah, upon the material interpretation of your redemption. Draw near in the holy quiet of the early morning, and let God show you that you are His. Let your faith in God rest quiet and wait upon Him until you receive the assurance, "I am His, whom He causes to draw near unto Him". This is what God will do for you in the early morning.

> Draw near in the holy quiet of the early morning, and let God show you that you are His.

11

Joshua And The Morning Watch

"And Joshua rose early in the morning, and the priests took up the ark of the Lord."

(Jos. 6:12, also Jos. 3:1, Jos. 7:16, Jos. 8:10.)

Four times Joshua is spoken of as rising up early in the morning, first at Shittim, where the people were about to pass over Jordan to take possession of the Promised Land; a second time at Jericho before compassing the walls of the city; then on the occasion of the discovery and punishment of the sin of Achan, and again at the capture of Ai. His early rising was the proof of his determination to do the work that God, from time to time, gave him to do. That determination was the proof of the strength of his trust in God to give Israel the victory, and the land of promise.

For many, in these days, who can find no quiet

moment in the middle of the day, early rising is of more importance to the spiritual life than perhaps they think. The word "early" does not convey the same meaning to everyone. But its meaning for all is that we must rise early enough to have some time alone with God. The conquest of the land of promise, the living of a strong life of faith, the discovery and extermination of secret sins, triumphant victory over enemies—all this is not achieved in idleness and ease. As Joshua rose up early to all those tasks that, as a servant of God, he might do God's all with undivided heart, so should it be with us. Let everyone, who longs to be like Joshua, a man of faith, and, like him, to receive the reward of faith, remember that it is written of him, "Joshua rose early in the morning."

11—*Joshua And The Morning Watch*

His early rising was the proof of his determination to do the work that God, from time to time, gave him to do...The conquest of the land of promise, the living of a strong life of faith, the discovery and extermination of secret sins, triumphant victory over enemies—all this is not achieved in idleness and ease... Let everyone, who longs to be like Joshua, a man of faith, and, like him, to receive the reward of faith, remember that it is written of him, "Joshua rose early in the morning."

12

The Light Of The Morning

"(There shall be) One that ruleth over men righteously, that ruleth in the fear of God. He shall be as the light of the morning, when the sun riseth, a morning without clouds, when the tender grass springeth out of the earth through clear shining after rain."

(2Sam. 23:3-4)

This is a prophecy of our Lord Jesus. To the soul under His governance He will be as the light of the morning. Nay, He Himself is the true light of the morning. "To you who fear My name shall the Sun of Righteousness arise with healing in His wings." Here may I learn to seek the full and true blessing of God in the morning. The sun that riseth in the morning gives light the whole day; were there no morning there could be no day.

12—*The Light Of The Morning*

When I find the Lord Jesus in the morning, and know Him as the Light of the morning that rises on my soul, there He will be the whole day, my Life and my Joy.

Soul! Be this thy task each morning. It is not reading or praying that brings blessing. The Lord Jesus must let His Light rise on your soul, and this He does by Faith. Apply yourself definitely to a quiet exercise of Faith. He will be, He is the morning Light. Receive by Faith the gentle beams of His love. Take Him, the Righteous Ruler, to rule over your soul. He will be to you every day as the Light of the morning when the sun riseth, a morning without clouds.

...Seek the full and true blessing of God in the morning. The sun that riseth in the morning gives light the whole day; were there no morning there could be no day.

13

Job And The Morning Watch

"And the sons of Job went and held a feast in the house of each one upon his day...And it was so...that Job sent and sanctified them and rose up early in the morning and offered burnt offerings...For Job said, It may be that my sons have sinned."

(Job 1:4-5.)

Here you have the ideal of a pious, God-fearing father. It is not enough for him to shun evil himself; he fears greatly that his children may perhaps sin against God. As the head of the household he sends and summons them to himself in order to sanctify them: He rises up early in the morning to offer burnt offerings for them. Splendid example of a pious father, and of the piety which does not serve God for itself alone, but also cares for the children.

Father! How do matters stand in your household? Are you faithful in taking your children to meet every morning around God's Word and in going with them to God in prayer? Oh, be sure to do it. Evening prayers are not enough. In the morning all is fresh; the morning is the beginning of the day, and influences the whole day. To prevent evil is better than to confess it when done. Let the whole household every morning begin the day with God, and receive God's blessing for the day.

Christian! If you wish to live each day and all the day as a child of God, be sure not to forget the solitary communion with God in the early morning. If you wish to have God's blessing in your house, do not forget morning prayers with your household.

13—Job And The Morning Watch

Father! How do matters stand in your household? Are you faithful in taking your children to meet every morning around God's Word and in going with them to God in prayer? Oh, be sure to do it. Evening prayers are not enough.

In the morning all is fresh; the morning is the beginning of the day, and influences the whole day.

14

A Visit From God Every Morning

"What is man, that Thou shouldst magnify him, and that Thou shouldst set Thy heart upon him, and that Thou shouldst visit him every morning, and try him every moment?"

(Job 7:17-18).

Soul! Hast thou ever known that God so magnifies thee, and has so set His heart upon thee, that He visits thee every morning? Hast thou learnt to prepare thyself every morning to receive that visit? Oh, do not, in haste or thoughtlessness, miss or despise so great a privilege—a visit every morning from thy God.

This means much more than reading and praying every morning. Much more. It means that God will give you, through His Spirit, the assurance that He remembers you in love, that He accepts you, that He will keep you, if you will but come before Him in the quiet exercise of faith which adores, awaits His presence. He will give you the heavenly assurance that He is with you. Only say: "My soul is still before God."

Job says: "What is man that Thou shouldst visit him every morning, and try him every moment?" How shall I be able to endure this? God trying me every moment in all the hurry and business of the day! There is only one way. I must await His visit in the morning. He desires to make a covenant with me for the day, and to give me anew into the keeping of His Son; then He can try me every moment.

Truly the man who receives a visit from his God every morning will gladly submit to be put to the test by Him every moment.

Job says: "What is man that Thou shouldst visit him every morning, and try him every moment?" How shall I be able to endure this? God trying me every moment in all the hurry and business of the day! There is only one way. I must await His visit in the morning.

15

Surely Now He Will Awake For Thee

"If thou wouldst seek unto God betimes, and make thy supplication to the Almighty; if thou wert pure and upright, surely now He would awake for thee...Though thy beginning was small, yet thy latter end shall greatly increase."

(Job 8:5-7)

One may seek God at any hour of the day; but to seek Him early is best. Seeking early is the proof that this is to us the first and most important work of the day. Seeking early helps the soul to wait upon God the whole day, and seeking early can lay claim to gracious promises.

If you awake early to seek God, God will awake early for your sake. If you seek Him early and make supplication to the Almighty, if you cast out sin and are pure and upright, "though thy beginning was small thy latter end shall greatly increase." It shall be with your soul as with the morning hours. The dawn begins with a few faint beams of light, but the light increases continually unto the perfect day. Your beginning, too, shall be small, the work of grace may be, at first, very feeble, but "thy latter end shall greatly increase." Only persevere in early seeking after God. Be alone with God, regularly, faithfully, morning after morning, without knowing how the blessing is going to come. You will grow stronger in the fear and the service of God, and in the love and joy of Christ. The God whom you seek early is a faithful God, "surely now He will awake for thee," and watch over thee in silence and work in thee, and" thy latter end shall greatly increase if thou wouldst seek unto God betimes."

15—Surely Now He Will Awake For Thee

If you awake early to seek God, God will awake early for your sake. If you seek Him early and make supplication to the Almighty, if you cast out sin and are pure and upright, "though thy beginning was small thy latter end shall greatly increase."

16

Thou Shalt Be As The Morning

"If thou prepare thine heart and stretch out thine hands toward Him, if iniquity be in thine hand, put it far away...then shalt thou lift up thy face without spot...thou shalt shine forth, thou shalt be as the morning."

(Job 11:13-17)

We have seen with what joy the Lord and His people commune together in the morning, and how well they understood how blessed a time the morning is.

We have seen that the morning is a symbol of Jesus Himself, "He shall be as a morning without clouds." Here we have a further promise: "the believer himself shall be as the morning."

What depth of meaning there is here! The meaning

is light after darkness. So shall be the life of the Christian. "Whoso cometh after me," said Jesus, "shall not walk in darkness, but shall have the light of life."

So morning is the beginning of a day which grows brighter and brighter. "The path of the just is as a shining light that shineth more and more unto the perfect day."

The morning diffuses gladness, awakening all around. This meaning, too, is intended by these words, "Thou shalt be as the morning".

And wouldst thou be as the morning, oh Christian? Learn from these words how thou mayest so become. "If thou prepare thine heart, and stretch out thine hands towards him," in prayer. Let not your prayer be without preparation of heart. Let the heart be quiet before God in the calm of the morning. Speak to God only after holy meditation. "My heart is fixed, Oh God, my heart is fixed." "If there be any iniquity in thine hand, put it far away"; lay aside every sin. "Thou shalt shine forth," as it were, upon the wings of the morning. "Thou shalt be as the morning." Oh, be faithful in giving the morning to God, and He will cause the morning to arise in you: He will grant to you to be as the morning.

AND WOULDST THOU BE AS THE MORNING, OH CHRISTIAN? LET NOT YOUR PRAYER BE WITHOUT PREPARATION OF HEART… "IF THOU PREPARE THINE HEART, AND STRETCH OUT THINE HANDS TOWARDS HIM,"… OH, BE FAITHFUL IN GIVING THE MORNING TO GOD, AND HE WILL CAUSE THE MORNING TO ARISE IN YOU!

17

My Voice Shalt Thou Hear In The Morning

"My voice shalt Thou hear in the morning. O Lord, in the morning will I direct my prayer unto Thee and will look up."

(Psalm 5:3)

David here gives expression to his intention that the morning shall continue to be the time when he will make his voice heard before God, and also to his confidence that God will, in reality, hearken to his voice. The morning is to be his time of exercise in prayer, and answer to prayer. Do thou, too, take these words and utter them in full confidence before God: "My voice shalt Thou hear in the morning."

"In the morning will I direct my prayer unto thee." This word "direct" is used of setting in order or preparing the dishes for a table (Exod. 40. 4), or it is the word for the offering upon an altar. Don't be in a hurry to kneel down and pray because you know how to compose a prayer. First "prepare to meet thy God." Sit down quietly for a few moments to form a right conception of God in His great Holiness. Call to mind with what fear and awe, with what truth and sincerity, and entire submission and obedience, it befits you to approach Him. Ask yourself if you have set your heart in order upon the altar, just as the offering was set in order upon the wood before it could be burnt. Say continually, "In the morning will I direct my prayer unto Thee."

"And look up" when you pray; do not neglect to look for God and His answer—to keep the watch of the Lord. This is the link between the morning prayer and the life of the day. "I wait upon Thee all the day," is the continuation and the blessing of intercourse with God in the morning. Therefore will I often say: "My voice shalt Thou hear in the morning, Oh Lord, in the morning will I direct my prayer unto Thee, and will look up."

"In the morning will I direct my prayer unto thee." This word "direct" is used of setting in order...Don't be in a hurry to kneel down and pray because you know how to compose a prayer. First "prepare to meet thy God."

18

Joyful Morning Prayer

"But I will sing of Thy power; yea, I will sing aloud of Thy mercy in the morning: for Thou hast been my defence and refuge in the day of my trouble."

(Psa. 59:16)

Here is the secret of joyful morning prayer. It is the thought of what God has done for the salvation of our souls, the experience that He has been to us a defence and a refuge.

If you long to glorify God's mercy in the morning as you ought, see to it first that you rightly know God as your defence and refuge. Read the words of David in which, with all his heart, he glorifies God as his fortress and refuge. (See Psa. 18:46 ; Psa. 62:2, Psa. 62:7-8 ; Psa. 142:2)

Pray this prayer continually: "Be Thou my strong habitation whereunto I may continually resort." (Psa. 71:3.) Say boldly: "I will say of the Lord, He is my refuge and fortress: my God, in Him will I trust." Almost before you are aware of it your soul will cry joyfully, "Under the shadow of Thy wings shall I sing with joy."

Christian, do not always meet your God in the morning with nothing but sighs! Let your faith look upon what He is to you, let your faith glory in Him—so shall you honour Him and obtain His favour. So shall your joyful morning sacrifice be the beginning of a day spent in the joy and strength which God alone gives.

Here is the secret of joyful morning prayer. It is the thought of what God has done for the salvation of our souls, the experience that He has been to us a defence and a refuge.

19

Early Will I Seek Thee

"O God, Thou art my God, early will I seek Thee, my soul thirsteth for Thee, my flesh longeth for Thee in a dry and thirsty land where no water is."

(Psa. 63:1.)

People constantly speak of themselves as seeking salvation. The Bible never speaks in this wise; as long as a man is only seeking salvation, he is still seeking his own interest himself. We must seek God, to possess Him is what we need. "I will seek Thee," says David.

What a wonderful salvation is that—when a man truly finds God, God Himself, not only forgiveness and peace, but finds and possesses God. When any man first sees the glory of it, no wonder that he then says: "...Early will I seek Thee."

Hedley Vicars, the godly soldier, when he knew that he must be at the head of his troops the following morning at five o'clock, rose an hour earlier to meet with his God, and so, too, did those brave soldiers Havelock and Stonewall Jackson.

Let this be the keynote of your morning solitude. Thirst for God, as the body thirsts for a drink of water. Be content with nothing short of finding and possessing God. Think of it! He desires to make His dwelling with you through His Son; His Spirit will be in you a fountain of living water. Seek and possess God—this is the only way in which He will reveal Himself to you. Make sacrifices to that end, your reward will be great. "Ye shall seek Me and find Me, when ye shall search for Me with all your heart."

Let this be the keynote of your morning solitude. Thirst for God, as the body thirsts for a drink of water. Be content with nothing short of finding and possessing God.

20

In The Morning Shall My Prayer Prevent Thee

"But unto Thee have I cried, O Lord; and in the morning shall my prayer prevent Thee."

(Psa. 88:13)

In this Psalm we find the writer in great darkness and distress. Prayer is his only comfort. "Oh, Lord God of my salvation, I have cried day and night before Thee" (vs. 1). "Lord, I have called daily upon Thee, I have stretched out my hands unto Thee" (Psa. 88:9). "Shall Thy wonders be known in the dark?" (Psa. 88:12). "But unto Thee have I cried, Oh Lord, and in the morning shall my prayer prevent Thee."

Are you, my reader, ever in darkness? Are you perhaps praying earnestly about something, and God does not seem to answer? Does it seem, in face of your wishes for yourself or for others, as if the Lord had forgotten to be gracious? Fear not! Take courage! Only believe! Say to Him: "In the morning shall my prayer prevent Thee." Don't go sighing the whole day before God; but let the fresh glad morning teach your faith a lesson, and give your prayer courage.

In the middle of the night all was dark as pitch, yet the light has come. The first rays of dawn were but a faint twilight, yet it is now light. And it will go on growing lighter until the full brightness of midday. Let God hear your voice in the morning. Cultivate a quiet confidence that He hears you, that He will not forget you throughout the day, and that an answer to your prayer is sure.

Are you perhaps praying earnestly about something, and God does not seem to answer? Does it seem, in face of your wishes for yourself or for others, as if the Lord had forgotten to be gracious? Fear not! Take courage! Only believe! Say to Him: "In the morning shall my prayer prevent Thee."

21

Thy Lovingkindness Is Better Than Life

"Cause me to hear Thy lovingkindness in the morning, for in Thee do I trust; cause me to know the way wherein I should walk, for I lift up my soul unto Thee."

(Psa. 143:8.)

On a previous occasion David had said: "Thy lovingkindness is better than life" (Psa. 63:3). When he awoke in the morning to the life of a new day, he instantly thought of what was better and more indispensable to him than life itself—the lovingkindness of God. Better be without life than without the lovingkindness of God.

Now what does he do to ensure this blessing? The answer is, that he gives the morning to God, he asks God to make him sensible of His lovingkindness; that is to say, he sets his heart open and waits quietly to hear what God has to say. This is something more than merely reading and praying in the morning. "Faith" is the ear with which we can "hear" God. Faith sits herself down quietly in the presence of God, and surrenders herself to the sense of His nearness. Faith prays the silent prayer: "Cause me to hear Thy lovingkindness, for in Thee do I trust," and in His Divine way the Lord accomplishes it; through the Holy Spirit He gives the soul a renewed assurance of His favour and good pleasure. By faith the soul receives the witness that it is well-pleasing with God. Blessed morn! When God causes us to hear His lovingkindness! And every morning may be like that. Now the soul may gladly utter the next prayer and expect an answer for the whole day: "Cause me. to know the way wherein I should walk, for I lift up my soul unto Thee."

21—Thy Lovingkindness Is Better Than Life

When [David] awoke in the morning to the life of a new day, he instantly thought of what was better and more indispensable to him than life itself—the lovingkindness of God... Blessed morn! When God causes us to hear His lovingkindness!

22

Satisfy Us Early With Thy Mercy

"O satisfy us early with Thy mercy, that we may rejoice and be glad all our days. Let Thy work appear unto Thy servants and Thy glory unto their children."

(Psa. 90:14, Psa. 90:16)

In our [previous] text the psalmist prays for himself alone: "Cause me to hear Thy lovingkindness." That was the morning prayer in solitude. Here he is praying both for himself and others: "Satisfy us with Thy mercy." In view of the mention of "children" almost immediately afterwards we may take this to be the prayer for the assembled household.

"Satisfy us with Thy mercy," says the petitioner. The father provides bread each morning for the children, and gives them as much as they need to satisfy them. To be satisfied means to have had enough, so that there is no more need. The believer desires, through faith and the Holy Ghost, to have such assurance of God's mercy that he is, as Moses said, "satisfied with favour and full with the blessing of the Lord" (Deut. 33:23.)

The father who wishes his children to be satisfied not only with bread but with the mercy of the Lord as their portion must first learn in solitude to pray the prayer: "Cause me to hear Thy lovingkindness in the morning." Then let him gather his household together every morning faithfully and lead them in believing prayer: "Let Thy work appear unto Thy servants and Thy glory unto their children. Satisfy us early with Thy mercy, that we may rejoice and be glad all our days."

Gather [your] household together every morning faithfully and lead them in believing prayer: "Let Thy work appear unto Thy servants and Thy glory unto [our] children. Satisfy us early with Thy mercy, that we may rejoice and be glad all our days."

23

Showing Forth His Lovingkindness In The Morning

"...It is a good thing to give thanks unto the Lord, and to sing praises unto Thy name, O Most High, to show forth Thy lovingkindness in the morning and Thy faithfulness every night."

(Psa. 92:1-2.)

How often we find the thought expressed that we must show forth God's lovingkindness in the morning! God has a right to it; it is He that has spared us and given us a new day. It will be a blessing to the soul; the glad remembrance and confession of God's lovingkindness brings with it the favour of the Lord.

To trust once more in His mercy supports and strengthens faith. It binds the soul to Him and His service in love and joy. It takes us out of ourselves and lifts us up to God. To praise God is a remedy for many diseases.

The question is: How do I come to be able to do it? Sin and weakness so often cast me down. Let me show you the way. The first step is: be sure to take time every morning for this duty; this will be proof to your God that you are really in earnest. Next sit down quietly before God and meditate on His love in Christ Jesus. Exercise a quiet faith in that wonderful love as resting upon you. And then begin to give thanks. Although you may not realize it all as clearly as you would like, although you have not many words, kneel down quietly and say with childlike confidence: "Father, I love Thee, and glorify Thy love. Thou lovest me, Amen. Hallelujah!"

To trust once more in His mercy supports and strengthens faith. It binds the soul to Him and His service in love and joy. It takes us out of ourselves and lifts us up to God. To praise God is a remedy for many diseases.

24

Seeking God Early

"With my soul have I desired Thee in the night, yea, with my spirit within me will I seek Thee early,"

(Isa. 26:9.)

Those that seek Me early shall find Me (Pro. 8:17.) If I am seeking for a treasure of great value, I am willing to go to much trouble for it. If the treasure is very hard to find, I shall not be able to attain my object unless I devote myself entirely to it. The treasure of Heaven is God Himself, infinite in worth, and to us, who are sinful and carnal, hard to find. Let us think no sacrifice too great if we may seek Him and truly find Him. Let us say to Him in the morning: "…Yea, with my spirit within me will I seek Thee early."

Then how can it be that a believer who has already found his God is still seeking God? Oh! God is so much greater than the little he yet knows and has of Him, that he may say with truth that he seeks completely to possess God in His completeness. He so needs a new revelation of God and His grace for the new day; he is so dependent on God's gift of Himself as free grace. God's gift of Himself to His child, and his possession of God through the Holy Spirit, may become so much deeper and stronger that he is constantly required to say: "…Thou art my God, in the morning will I seek Thee, my soul thirsteth for Thee." Therefore, too, he says: "…With my spirit within me will I seek Thee early." This "spirit" is the hidden dwelling and sphere of the Holy Spirit. He sets the heart wide open so that God may take possession of it and fill it with Himself wholly.

How can it be that a believer who has already found his God is still seeking God? Oh! God is so much greater than the little he yet knows and has of Him, that he may say with truth that he seeks completely to possess God in His completeness.

25

Be Thou My Arm Every Morning

"O Lord, be gracious unto us; we have waited for Thee; be Thou their arm every morning, our salvation also in the time of trouble."

(Isa. 33:2)

When a man in business is not possessed of much means himself, but has a wealthy friend to render him financial support, it is sometimes said: "He has a strong arm in that friend." In the Scriptures we read: "Thou hast an arm of power", "The Lord hath sworn by the arm of His strength, "In My arm shall they hope." And here we have the prayer: "Lord, be gracious unto us, we have waited for Thee: be Thou their arm every morning, our salvation also in the time of trouble."

What a blessed thing it is, when the believer takes time every morning to pray that prayer, so as not to go forth to the temptation and strife of the day until he first has the living assurance that his prayer: "Be Thou my arm in the morning", has been heard, and that God is really the strong arm supporting him! Christian, take pains every morning to grasp this fact. Then you will understand the meaning of the words: "Neither did their own arm save them, but Thy right hand and Thine arm." (Psa. 44:3.)

But to this end it is necessary to say first: "We have waited for Thee." God is a Spirit, and can only be known spiritually. The Holy Spirit must show us Him and His strong right arm. He must teach us wholly to mistrust our own arm and our own strength, and truly by faith to take God's arm instead of ours. He will do this for everyone who waits for Him. So shall God be "their arm every morning."

25—Be Thou My Arm Every Morning

"Be thou my arm in the morning"...Christian, take pains every morning to grasp this fact. Then you will understand the meaning of the words: "Neither did their own arm save them, but Thy right hand and Thine arm."

26

Awaken Mine Ear Every Morning

"The Lord God hath given me the tongue of the learned, that I should know how to speak a word in season to him that is weary; He awakeneth morning by morning, He awakeneth mine ear to hear as the learned."

(Isa. 1:4)

Thus speaks the prophet of himself as a type of the Lord Jesus. Thus speaks the Lord Jesus. Thus every believer may, and must speak, for all shall be taught. (Isa. 54:13 ; John 6:45.)

And how does God teach His children? "He awakeneth morning by morning; he awakeneth mine ear to hear as the learned." What God does is to arouse the ear—the faculty of listening. He teaches the soul to be quiet and listen to His voice. Much speaking and little listening, much prayer and little waiting, bring but little blessing. Faith is the ear that listens for God. The soul that waits quietly and is willing not only to pray, but (what is more important) to listen faithfully to what God is saying to the heart through His Spirit, will in truth be taught of God.

It is especially in the morning that God awakens the ear. He begins early in the day. He wants to be the first.

He awakeneth "morning by morning: He awakeneth mine ear." The Lord knows that we need fresh manna every morning. It is only by the daily renewal and repetition of our lesson that we are truly taught of God.

Soul! Let God awaken your ear each morning to listen to Him.

Much speaking and little listening, much prayer and little waiting, bring but little blessing...The soul that waits quietly and is willing not only to pray, but to listen faithfully to what God is saying to the heart through His Spirit, will in truth be taught of God.

27

New Mercies Every Morning

"It is of the Lord's mercies that we are not consumed, because His compassions fail not. They are new every morning: great is Thy faithfulness."

(Lam. 3:22-23.)

In the Psalms we often find mention made of the mercies of the Lord in connection especially with the morning. Sometimes it is a prayer. "Make me to hear Thy lovingkindness," or "satisfy us with Thy mercy." Sometimes, again it is of a "joyful song," or "the showing forth of Thy mercy," that the Psalmist speaks, but, whatever it may be, it is in the morning. Our text [here] tells us the reason: "because His compassions...are new every morning." What, then, more natural, more reasonable, than to praise for them every morning? Those of you who are parents, who have perhaps, hitherto, been content merely to give thanks and offer up prayer to God in private, delay no longer, but begin at once to gather your household together for that purpose.

Although it may be hard to begin, it will soon become easier. Let the whole household assemble to acknowledge God's mercy and beseech His aid during the day. Let God's Word be listened to with reverence as the revelation of His love and His will. Let His praise be sung and His Name be called upon. Teach every child, so far as it is in your power, to acknowledge the mercies of God every morning; it may be a blessing for the whole life and for eternity.

Do not forget; the Lord's mercies are new every morning. They must be praised for anew every morning.

27—New Mercies Every Morning

DO NOT FORGET; THE LORD'S MERCIES ARE NEW EVERY MORNING. THEY MUST BE PRAISED FOR ANEW EVERY MORNING.

28

The Just Lord and His Judgments Every Morning

"The just Lord is in the midst thereof; He will not do iniquity; every morning doth He bring His judgment to light."

(Zeph. 3:5.)

As the Almighty Lord, God is the Governor of this world, and faithfully, without fail, He gives anew every morning the light of the sun to illumine the world. As the "just Lord" He is .. in the midst" of His people, and "every morning doth He bring His judgment to light." As certainly as God gives the light of the sun every morning, does He also bring His judgments to light. "I shall make my judgment to lighten the nations."

God will do this every morning. In His Word we have His judgments (Ps. 119:102, 106, 108). Every morning He Himself brings His judgment to light and causes the light of His countenance and His Spirit to shine upon His Law that the people may understand and keep it. Only I must apply myself each morning to do two things. First I must take God's judgments in His Word and obey them and write them in my heart; and, second, I must wait upon God every morning until He brings His judgments to light—until His light is shed upon my soul. Only in the light of God's countenance and His love can His Word be rightly understood and truly kept.

Christian! Think deeply on what God will do for you each morning. Every morning He brings His judgments to light. Let this be the chief part of your morning devotions—waiting upon God until He sheds His light upon your soul. So will you gain wisdom and strength for the day.

I MUST WAIT UPON GOD EVERY MORNING UNTIL HE BRINGS HIS JUDGMENTS TO LIGHT—UNTIL HIS LIGHT IS SHED UPON MY SOUL.

29

Secret Communion With God

"And in the morning, rising up a great while before day, He went out and departed into a solitary place and there prayed."

(Mark 1:35)

We have seen in the Old Testament what a series there was of men of God to whom it is said that they rose up early to do God's will, to meet Him, or seek His favour. This series is brought to a conclusion by the Lord Jesus. After a busy and toilsome day (v. 34), a day of constant intercourse with men, a day in which He had to give much of Himself, He felt the need of closer communion with God, in order to renew His strength and receive further guidance in His work. "A great while before day"—while it was yet night—rising up, "He went out and departed into a solitary place and there prayed."

If the Son of God needed to do that, how much more do we? Not only in the midst of business and worldly occupation, but also in times of spiritual exertion, secret communion with God is indispensable.

You, Christian, are a follower of Christ; follow Him in this also. The mind which was in Christ is also in you. He will wake you, too, out of sleep to go out and pray alone. Jesus did not rise every morning while it was yet night—there are times of special need. But what we do need every morning is a real personal meeting with the Living God. Let us not lose sight of this; without early rising the Son of God could not fulfil His life work. May it be for us, as for Him, a part of our life in God!

...In times of spiritual exertion, secret communion with God is indispensable. What we need every morning is a real personal meeting with the Living God. Let us not lose sight of this; without early rising the Son of God could not fulfil His life work.

30

Great Lessons Spring From The Morning Watch

"And at night He went out and abode in the mount that is called the Mount of Olives. And all the people came early in the morning to Him in the Temple for to hear Him."

(Luke 21:37-38)

"And in the morning, as they passed by, they saw the fig tree dried up from the roots...And Jesus, answering, saith unto them, Have faith in God."

(Mark 11:20, Mark 11:22.)

It was toward the end of His life, when the Passion was drawing near, that the Lord spent the night on the Mount of Olives, and then came back to the city in the early morning, where the people came to Him. It was on one of these days that, early in the morning, He uttered the glorious words: "Have faith in God," with the famous words concerning "removing mountains," and the promise, "What things soever ye desire, when ye pray, believe that ye receive them and ye shall have them."

Oh that all, who say they love Jesus, and who complain that they have so much to do in the daytime, might know what a blessing it is to come in the morning early and be taught of Him. What a lesson the disciples would have missed, had they not been with Jesus early that morning! How much we miss because we have no time to listen in the morning when the Lord visits us and waits for us! The lesson of the true meaning of those words, "What things soever ye desire, when ye pray..." will be taught to those who, with faithful perseverance, seek to learn from Jesus in the morning.

In the morning early, Oh my soul, thou canst especially reckon on the teaching of thy Lord.

...What a blessing it is to come in the morning early and be taught of Him...How much we miss because we have no time to listen in the morning when the Lord visits us and waits for us!

31

The Secret Of Early Rising

"And very early in the morning, the first day of the week, they came unto the sepulchre at the rising of the sun...Now when Jesus was risen early the first day of the week, He appeared first to Mary Magdalene out of whom He had cast seven devils."

(Mark 16:2, 9)

The women went to the grave early in the morning. But Jesus was there before them and awaited them. He was risen when it was still very early. Mary had gone first, "early, when it was yet dark" (John xx. I), and first of all the Lord appeared unto her. The living Jesus who awaiteth us early, and who visits us every morning, and the believing soul that riseth early to seek Him, these will certainly meet each other.

And what was the secret cause of that early rising of Mary and the other women? It was their love for Jesus. They could not find rest away from Him, His presence was indispensable to them. Such love as theirs He could not disappoint.

And all ye who rise early, and yet do not know that Jesus requires the morning, think of the blessing you will miss; the living Lord speaketh: "Those that seek Me early shall find me."

And ye who know and seek the Lord, and yet acknowledge that you do not love Him sufficiently, because you do not have sufficient communion with the living Saviour, do realize the blessing prepared for you, if you are ready to make the needful sacrifice of seeking Him early in the morning. It will be your portion to walk in the light and the power of the Risen Saviour day by day and during the course of each day.

31—The Secret Of Early Rising

THE WOMEN WENT TO THE GRAVE EARLY IN THE MORNING. BUT JESUS WAS THERE BEFORE THEM AND AWAITED THEM...THE LIVING JESUS WHO AWAITETH US EARLY, AND WHO VISITS US EVERY MORNING, AND THE BELIEVING SOUL THAT RISETH EARLY TO SEEK HIM, THESE WILL CERTAINLY MEET EACH OTHER.

32

The Morning Watch in the Life of Obedience.

If the first fruit is holy, so is the lump; and if the root is holy, so are the branches.

Rom. 11:16.

How wonderful and blessed is the divine appointment of the first day of the week as a holy day of rest. Not, (as some think), that we might have at least one day of rest and spiritual refreshment amid the weariness of life, but that that one holy day, at the opening of the week, might sanctify the whole, might help and fit us to carry God's holy presence into all the week and its work. With the first-fruit holy, the whole lump is holy; with the root holy, all the branches are holy too.

How gracious, too, the provision suggested by so

many types and examples of the Old Testament, by which a morning hour at the opening of the day can enable us to secure a blessing for all its work, and give us the assurance of

POWER FOR VICTORY OVER EVERY TEMPTATION.

How unspeakably gracious, that in the morning hour the bond that unites us with God can be so firmly tied that during hours when we have to move amid the rush of men or duties, and can scarce think of God, the soul can be kept safe and pure; that the soul can so give itself away, in the time of secret worship, into His keeping, that temptation shall only help us to unite it closer with Him. What cause for praise and joy, that the morning watch can so each day renew and strengthen the surrender to Jesus and the faith in Him, that the life of obedience can not only be maintained in fresh vigor, but can indeed go on from strength to strength.

I would fain point out how intimate and vital the connection between obedience and the morning watch is. The desire for a life of entire obedience will give new meaning and value to the morning watch, even as this again can alone give the strength and courage needed for the former.

I. THE MOTIVE PRINCIPLE.

Think first of the motive principle that will make us love and faithfully keep the morning watch.

If we take it upon us simply as a duty, and a necessary part of our religious life, it will very soon become a burden. Or, if the chief thought be our own happiness and safety, that will not supply the power to make it truly attractive. There is only one thing will suffice—the desire for fellowship with God.

It is for that we were created in God's likeness. It is that in which we hope to spend eternity. It is that alone can fit us for a true and blessed life, either here, or hereafter. To have more of God, to know Him better, to receive from Him the communication of His love and strength, to have our life filled with His,-it is for this He invites us to enter the inner chamber and shut the door.

It is in the closet, in the morning watch, that our spiritual life is both tested and strengthened. There is the battlefield where it is to be decided every day whether God is to have all, whether our life is to be absolute obedience. If we truly conquer there, getting rid of ourselves into the hands of our Almighty Lord, the victory during the day is sure. It is there, in the inner chamber, proof is to be given whether we really delight in God, and make it our aim to love Him with our whole heart.

Let this, then, be our first lesson: the presence of God is the chief thing, in our devotions. To meet God, to give ourselves into His holy will, to know that we are pleasing to Him, to have Him give us our orders, and lay His hand upon us, and bless us, and say to us, 'Go in this thy strength'-it is when the soul learns that this is what is to be found in the morning watch, day by day, that we shall learn to long for it and delight in it.

II. READING THE BIBLE.

Let us next speak of the reading of God's Word, as part of what occupies us there. With regard to this I have more than one thing I wish to say.

1. One is that unless we beware, the Word, which is meant to point us away to God, may actually intervene and hide Him from us.

The mind may be occupied and interested and delighted at what it finds, and yet, because this is more head knowledge than anything else, it may bring little good to us. If it does not lead us to wait on God, to glorify Him, to receive His grace and power for sweetening and sanctifying our lives, it becomes a hindrance instead of a help.

2. Another lesson that cannot be repeated too often, or pressed too urgently, is that it is only by the teaching of the Holy Ghost that we can get at the real meaning of what God means by His Word, and that the Word will really reach into our inner life, and work in us.

The Father in heaven, who gave us His Word from heaven, with its divine mysteries and message, has given us His Holy Spirit in us, to explain and internally appropriate that Word. The Father wants us each time to ask that He teach us by His Spirit. He wants us to bow in a meek, teachable frame of mind, and believe that the Spirit will, in the hidden depth of our heart, make His Word live and work. He wants us to remember that the Spirit is given us that we should be led by Him, should walk after Him, should have our whole life under His rule, and that therefore He cannot teach us in the morning unless we honestly give up ourselves to His leading. But if we do this and patiently wait on Him, not to get new thoughts but to get the power of the Word in our heart, we can count upon His teaching.

Let your closet be the classroom, let your morning watch be the study hour, in which your relation of entire dependence on, and submission to, the Holy

Spirit's teaching is proved to God.

3. A third remark I want to make, in confirmation of what was said above, is this: ever study in God's Word in the spirit of an unreserved surrender to obey.

You know how often Christ, and His apostles in their Epistles, speak of hearing and not doing. If you accustom yourself to study the Bible without an earnest and very definite purpose to obey, you are getting hardened in disobedience.

Never read God's will concerning you without honestly giving up yourself to do it at once, and asking grace to do so. God has given us His Word, to tell us what He wants us to do and what grace He has provided to enable us to do it: how sad to think it a pious thing just to read that Word without any earnest effort to obey it! May God keep us from this terrible sin!

Let us make it a sacred habit to say to God, 'Lord, whatever I know to be Thy will, I will at once obey.' Ever read with a heart yielded up in willing obedience.

4. One more remark. I have here spoken of such commands as we already know, and as are easily understood. But, remember, there are a great many

commands to which your attention may never have been directed, or others of which the application is so wide and unceasing that you have not taken it in. Read God's Word with a deep desire to know all His will. If there are things which appear difficult, commands which look too high, or for which you need a divine guidance to tell you how to carry them out,-and there are many such,-let them drive you to seek a divine teaching. It is not the text that is easiest and most encouraging that brings most blessing, but the text, whether easy or difficult, which throws you most upon God. God would have you 'filled with the knowledge of His will in all wisdom and spiritual understanding'; it is in the closet this wonderful work is to be done. Do remember, it is only when you know that God is telling you to do a thing that you feel sure He gives the strength to do it. It is only as we are willing to know all God's will that, He will from time to time reveal more of it to us, and that we, will be able to do it all.

What a power the morning watch may be in the life of one who makes a determined resolve to meet God there; to renew the surrender to absolute obedience; humbly and patiently to wait on the Holy Spirit to be taught all God's will; and to receive the assurance that every promise given him in the Word will infallibly be made true! He that thus prays for himself, will become a true intercessor for others.

III. PRAYER.

It is in the light of these thoughts I want now to say a few words on what prayer is to be in the morning watch.

1. First of all, see that you secure the presence of God.

Do not be content with anything less than seeing the face of God, having the assurance that He is looking on you in love, and listening and working in you.

If our daily life is to be full of God, how much more the morning hour, where the life of the day alone can have God's seal stamped upon it. In our religion we want nothing so much as MORE OF GOD- His love, His will, His holiness, His Spirit living in us, His power working in us for men. Under heaven there is no way of getting this but by close personal communion. And there is no time so good for securing and practicing it, as the morning watch.

The superficiality and feebleness of our religion and religious work all come from having so little real contact with God. If it be true that God alone is the fountain of all love and good and happiness, and that to have as much as possible of His presence and His fellowship, of His will and His service, is our truest and highest happiness, surely then to meet Himself alone in the morning watch ought to be

OUR FIRST CARE.

To have had God appear to them, and speak to them, was with all the Old Testament saints the secret of their obedience and their strength. Do give God time in secret so to reveal Himself, that your soul may call the name of the place Peniel,-'for I have seen Him face to face.'

2. My next thought is: let the renewal of your surrender to absolute obedience for that day be a chief part of your morning sacrifice.

Let any confession of sin be very definite-a plucking out and cutting off of everything that has been grieving to God. Let any prayer for grace for a holy walk be as definite-an asking and accepting in faith of the very grace and strength you are specially in need of. Let your outlook on the day you are entering on be a very determined resolve that obedience to God shall be

ITS CONTROLLING PRINCIPLE.

Do understand that there is no surer way, rather, that there is no other possible way, of getting into God's love and blessing in prayer, than by getting into His will. In prayer, give up yourself most absolutely to the blessed will of God: this will avail more than much asking. Beseech God to show you this great mercy, that He allows you, that He will enable you, to enter into His will, and abide there-that will make the knowing and doing His will in your life a blessed certainty. Let your prayer indeed be a 'morning sacrifice,' a placing yourself as a whole burnt-offering on the altar of the Lord.

The measure of surrender to full obedience will be the measure of confidence toward God.

3. Then remember that true prayer and fellowship with God cannot be all from one side.

We need to be still, to wait and hear what response God gives. This is the office of the Holy Spirit, to be the voice of God to us. In the hidden depths of the heart, He can give a secret but most certain assurance that we are heard, that we are well-pleasing, that the Father engages to do for us what we have asked. What we need, to hear the Voice, to receive this assurance, is the quiet stillness that waits on God, the quiet faith that trusts in God, the quiet heart that bows in nothingness and humility before God, and allows Him to be all in all.

It is when God is waited on to take His part in our prayer that the confidence will come to us that we receive what we ask, that our surrender of ourselves in the sacrifice of obedience is accepted, and that therefore we can count upon the Holy Spirit to guide us into all the will of God, as He means us to know and do it.

What glory would come to us in the morning watch, and through it into our daily life, if it were thus made an hour spent with the Triune God, for the Father, through the Son and the Spirit, to take conscious possession of us for the day. How little need there then would be to urge and plead with God's children to watch the morning watch!

4. And now comes the last and the best of all. Let your prayer be intercessional, on behalf of others.

In the obedience of our Lord Jesus, as in all His fellowship with the Father, the essential element was-it was all for others. This Spirit flows though every member of the body; the more we know it, and yield to it, the more will our life be what God would make it. The highest form of prayer is intercession. The chief object for which God chose Abraham and Israel and us was to make us a blessing to the world. We are a royal priesthood-a priestly people. As long as prayer is only a means of personal improvement and happiness, we cannot know its full power. Let intercession be a real longing for the souls of those around us, a real bearing of the burden of their sin and need, a real pleading for the extension of God's kingdom, real labor in prayer for definite purposes to be realized-let such intercession be what the morning watch is consecrated to, and see what new interest and attraction it will have.

Intercession! Oh to realize what it means! To take the name, and the righteousness, and the worthiness of Christ, to put them on, and in them to appear before God! 'In Christ's stead,' now that He is no longer in the world, to beseech God, by name, for the individual men and needs, where His grace can do its work! In the faith of our own acceptance, and of the anointing with the Spirit to fit us for the work, to know that our prayer can avail to 'save a soul from death,' can bring down and dispense the blessing of heaven upon earth! To think that in the hour of the morning watch this work can be renewed and carried on day by day, each inner chamber maintaining its own separate communication with heaven, and helping together in bringing down its share of the blessing.

It is in intercession, more than in the zeal that works in its own strength with little prayer, that the highest type of piety, the true Christlikeness is cultivated. It is in intercession that a believer rises to his true nobility in the power of imparting life and blessing. It is to intercession we must look for any large increase of the power of God in the Church and its work for men.

One word in conclusion. Turn back and think now again about

THE INTIMATE AND VITAL CONNECTION

between obedience and the morning watch.

Without obedience there cannot be the spiritual power to enter into the knowledge of God's Word and will. Without obedience there cannot be the confidence, the boldness, the liberty that knows that it is heard. Obedience is fellowship with God in His will; without it there is not the capacity for seeing and claiming and holding the blessings He has for us.

And so, on the other side, without very definite living communion with God in the morning watch, the life of obedience cannot possibly be maintained. It is there that the vow of obedience can every morning be renewed in power and confirmed from above. It is there that the presence and fellowship can be secured which make obedience possible. It is there that in the obedience of the One, and in the union with Himself, the strength is received for all that God can ask. It is there that the spiritual understanding of God's will is received, which leads to walk worthy of the Lord to all well-pleasing.

God has called His children to live a wonderful, heavenly, altogether supernatural life. Let the morning watch each day be to you as

THE OPEN GATE OF HEAVEN,

through which its light and power streams in on your waiting heart, and from which you go out to walk with God all the day.

EPILOGUE

NOTES ON THE MORNING WATCH.

'By the observance of the morning watch is commonly meant the spending of at least the first half-hour of every day alone with God, in personal devotional Bible study and prayer.'

'There are Christians who say that they do not have time to devote a full half-hour to such a spiritual exercise. It is a striking fact that the busiest Christians constitute the class who plead this excuse the least, and most generally observe the morning watch. Any Christian who will honestly and persistently follow this plan for a month or two will become convinced that it is the best possible use of his time, that it does not interfere with his regular work, and that it promotes the wisest economy of time...'

EPILOGUE—*Notes On The Morning Watch.*

'In India, in China, in Japan, hundreds of students have agreed to keep the morning watch....'

'The practical question for each of us is, Why should not I keep the morning watch? Next to receiving Christ as Savior, and claiming the baptism of the Holy Ghost, we know of no act attended with larger good to ourselves and to others than the formation of an undiscourageable resolution to keep the morning watch.'

These quotations are from an address by John R. Mott. At first sight the closing statement appears too strong. But think a moment, what such a revelation implies.

It means the deep conviction that the only way to maintain and carry out the surrender to Christ and the Holy Spirit, is by meeting God very definitely at the commencement of each day, and receiving from Himself the grace needed for a walk in holy obedience.

It means an insight into the folly of attempting to live a heavenly life without rising up into close communion with God in heaven, and receiving from Himself the fresh bestowal of spiritual blessings.

It means the confession that it is alone in personal fellowship with God, and in delight in His nearness, that proof can be given that our love responds to His, and that we count His nearness our chief joy.

It means the faith that if time enough be given for God to lay His hands on us, and renew the inflowings of His Spirit, our soul may be so closely united to Him that no trials or duties can separate us from Him.

It means a purpose to live wholly and only for God, and by the sacrifice of time and ease to prove that we are willing to pay any price to secure the first of all blessings the presence of God for all the day.

Let us now look again at that sentence—'Next to receiving Christ as our Savior, and claiming the baptism of the Holy Spirit, we know of no act attended with larger good to ourselves or to others than the formation of an undiscourageable resolution to keep the morning watch.' If our acceptance of Christ as Lord and Master was whole-hearted, if our prayer for and claiming of the Holy Spirit to guide and control was sincere, surely there can be no thought of not giving God each day sufficient time,

EPILOGUE—*Notes On The Morning Watch.*

our very best time, for receiving and increasing in us what is indispensable to a life for Christ's glory and in His service.

You tell me there are many Christians who are content with ten minutes or a quarter of an hour. There are, but you will certainly not as a rule find them strong Christians. And the Students' Movement is pleading with God, above everything, that He would meet to train a race of devoted, whole-hearted young men and women. Christ asked great sacrifices of His disciples; He has perhaps asked little of you as yet. But now He allows, He invites, He longs for you to make some. Sacrifices make strong men. Sacrifices help wonderfully to wrench us away from earth and self-pleasing, and lift us heavenward. Do not try to pare down the time limit of the morning watch to less than the half-hour. There can be no question about the possibility of finding the time. Ten minutes from sleep, ten from company or amusement ,ten from lessons. How easy where the heart is right, hungering to know God and His will perfectly!

If you feel that you do not feel the need of so much time, and know not how to wait, we are content you should speak of your quiet time, or your hour of prayer. God may graciously, later on, draw you out to the morning watch. But do not undertake it unless you feel your heart stirred with the determination to make a sacrifice, and have full time for intimate intercourse with God. But if you are ready to do this, we urge you to join. The very fact of setting apart such a period helps to awaken the feeling: I have a great work to do, and I need time for it. It strengthens in your heart the conviction: If I am to be kept all this day without sin I must have time to get near to God. It will give your Bible study new point, as you find time, between the reading, to be still and bow in humility for the Holy Spirit's hidden working, and wait till you get some real apprehension of God's will for you, through the Word. And, by the grace of God, it may help you to begin that habit of specific and definite intercession of which the Church so surely stands in need.

Students! You know not whether in your future life your time may be more limited, your circumstances more unfavorable, your Christian earnestness feebler. Now is the accepted time. Today, as the Holy Ghost saith. Listen to the invitation of your brethren in all lands, and fear not to form an undiscourageable resolution to spend at least half an hour each morning with God alone.

ABOUT THE AUTHOR

Biography of Andrew Murray

Andrew Murray was born on May 9th, 1828 in Graaff Reinet, South Africa. Murray had an incredible Christian heritage growing up. His father was a Dutch Reformed minister who weekly read revival accounts to his family, and prayed regularly for revival to come to South Africa. Missionaries traveled through constantly, including David Livingston.

In 1838, when Murray was ten, he and his brother John went to study in Scotland. They went to train with their uncle, the Rev. John Murray. In the spring of 1840 the revivalist William C. Burns came and spoke in Aberdeen, Scotland. Burns made a deep impression Andrew. He was staying at his uncle's house and they spent long evenings sharing about the work of God. Burns had been instrumental in the great Kilsyth Revival of 1839. His heart was constantly broken over the lost, and he would weep and pray for hours for their salvation. Andrew would listen, with awe, as Burns would preach, and he saw a model of what he would like to become. Andrew and John attended Marischal College and graduated in 1844.

The two brothers then went to Utrecht, Holland, for further theological studies. They became part of a zealous group called "Sechor Dabar" (Remember the Word). Here they found others with the same passion for the lost and the Word of God. News reached them of the revival going on in Mottlingen, Germany led by Johann Blumhardt. It had started through an extraordinary deliverance and led to revival, healing, and miracles. Andrew and John went to meet with him and "saw firsthand the ongoing work of God's power in his own time."

In 1848 the two brothers were ordained and went back to South Africa. Andrew had a traveling ministry, where he would go out on horseback, for weeks at a time, to hold meetings for the Dutch-speaking South African farmers. It was a time of deep introspection and development of his fire for prayer and the gospel. In 1856 he married Emma Rutherford, the daughter of an English pastor. In 1860 Andrew accepted a pastorate in Worcester. He came, to the church, at the same time as a scheduled conference on revival and missions. Some of what was shared was about the revivals in North America and Europe. The cry of the pastors was that revival would also break out in South Africa. Revival did break out, but not in the way Andrew expected. It seemed out of order, but God impressed upon Andrew that it was His work. Andrew had a completely different view of revival after that experience. In 1877 he traveled to the United States and spoke at holiness conventions all over the country.

Murray's life was preaching and teaching. Then tragedy struck. In 1879 he became ill and his throat was impacted. He lost his voice and began the two "silent years". These years molded Murray in a new way. He surrendered everything to God. He came to a place of deep humility and love for God and for others. He met with Otto Stockmayer to get a deeper understanding of the theology of healing. In 1881 he went to London to Bethshan, a faith cure home started by W. E. Boardman. He was completely healed there and never had trouble with his throat again. From that point on he knew that the gifts of God were for believers today, and taught and wrote about it. In 1882 he attended the Keswick Convention. This convention emphasized "Holiness" and "Deeper Life" themes. Eventually, in 1895, he became a featured speaker.

Murray began an extensive schedule of traveling and

speaking. Twice he was in car accidents that left him with a limp. These God chose not to heal. Eventually he focused on writing books, as he was a prolific writer. Between 1858 and 1917 he wrote over 240 books. Many of these are considered classics and are still in print today. His books have touched a multitude of people drawing them On January 18th, 1917, Andrew Murray died praising God.

Source: Healing and Revival Press < http://healing andrevival.com/BioAMurray.htm > Used by permission.

Made in the USA
Middletown, DE
30 April 2018